TEX-MEX TAKEOUT RECIPE

Homemade Tex-Mex Recipes You Should Try (2022 Cookbook for Beginners)

Darren Ray

1

TABLE OF CONTENTS

INTRODUCTION

The iconic dishes of Tex-Mex cuisine include chilli con Carne, fajitas, tacos, and nachos. These are well-known dishes that many people consider to be comfort food. TexMex, short for Texan-Mexican, is an exciting mix of flavours and spices from Mexican, Spanish, Native American, and Berber influences passed down through tradition over several centuries, similar to other cuisines adopted into American culture. It is a dynamic cuisine that is constantly evolving and incorporating new flavours, gracefully adapting to changing tastes and needs.

Tejanos' traditions, mostly descended from Spanish settlers in what is now modern Texas, maybe the earliest origins of Tex-Mex cuisine. People from the Canary Islands were brought in by the Spaniards around the 1700s and influenced Tejano cooking with Berber spices such as cumin, chilli, and garlic. Northern Mexican cuisine began to gain popularity with the arrival of Mexican immigrants in the 1950s, inevitably blending with Texan flavours. Although the term "Tex-Mex" is said to have been coined in the 1940s to refer to Mexican dishes prepared by Texan cooks, Americans still referred to it simply as Mexican food. Diana Kennedy, the author of Cuisines of Mexico, began to distinguish between authentic Mexican and American-Mexican dishes in 1972, referring to the latter as Tex-Mex. Some people consider Mexican-influenced dishes in Arizona, New Mexico, and parts of California to be part of Tex-Mex cuisine.

Signature Tex-Mex dishes, which are commonly assumed to be Mexican, were invented in the United States. Chili con carne, for example, arose from the abundance of beef enjoyed by Texan cowboys. A German immigrant invented the chilli powder used in this concoction in Texas in the 1890s. Chimichangas were created in the 1950s in Tucson, Arizona. Nachos first appeared in Dallas in 1964, and fajitas, as we know them today, originated in Houston in 1973.

3

Some consider Tex-Mex to be an American regional cuisine today. It is a native cuisine influenced by foreign flavours, a Texan take on Mexican food, or a fusion of Mexican and cowboy fare. Since the 1970s, it has grown in popularity throughout the world, beginning in Paris and spreading throughout Europe, Asia, and the rest of the world. Tex-Mex is gradually incorporating authentic Mexican dishes, serving both types side by side in restaurants, as American palates begin to appreciate foreign flavours. It could also be argued that Mexicans are beginning to accept Tex-Mex in their culinary traditions. Other Latin American dishes are slowly making their way into Tex-Mex restaurants and establishing themselves as a part of American regional cooking. Tex-Mex cuisine, which began as poor man's street food, has now transcended class boundaries and appeals to people from all walks of life.

Tex-Mex Cooking Ingredients

The ingredients used are said to be what distinguishes Tex-Mex from true Mexican cuisine. Tex-Mex uses a limited number of ingredients, the majority of which are rarely found in authentic Mexican cuisine.

Beans

Beans are a popular ingredient in Tex-Mex dishes. Because pinto beans are plentiful in the United States, they are frequently refried or used as a filling for burritos. Small red beans, kidney beans, navy beans, or black-eyed peas are some of the most common beans used in chilli con Carne, Texas' official dish and an iconic Tex-Mex dish.

Cheese

Cheddar or yellow cheese is the most common and truly American ingredient, dating back to the days when Velveeta provided convenience to both home and restaurant cooks. It's typically slathered on nachos, used as a filling for enchiladas, or as the main ingredient in queso dip.

Chipotle Powder

A Texan concoction was invented in 1896 by a German immigrant.

Traditional ingredients include dried chillies, oregano, cumin, garlic, and salt. Some attribute this powder's Tex-Mex identity to it.

Cumin

Except in the northern parts of the country, cumin is rarely used in Mexico. It was said that early Tejanos were introduced to it by Canary Islanders. It contributes to the distinct flavour of chilli con Carne.

Jalapenos

Texas' mildly pungent state pepper is perhaps the most commonly used in Tex-Mex cuisine. It is used in the preparation of salsa, chillies, and pickles, as well as a garnish for many dishes. Chipotles are jalapenos that have been smoked. (NOTE: After handling jalapenos, keep your hands away from your eyes and sensitive areas on your face!)

Lettuce

This is used as a side dish or as one of the main ingredients in many Tex-Mex dishes. It is uncommon in authentic Mexican dishes.

Meat

Ground beef is commonly used in Tex-Mex dishes because it is what Texan cowboys ate. Ground beef is not the only meat used. Chicken and pork are also used, but not as frequently.

The sour cream

Another authentically American ingredient was presumably added as a replacement for Mexican crema, which is thinner and less sour.

Tomato

Tex-Mex chefs used canned tomatoes in their dishes because they were easy to use. The base of most sauces is tomato sauce or tomato paste.

Flour made from wheat

Instead of maize flour, which is more commonly used in traditional Mexican tortillas, wheat flour is the main ingredient used to make tortillas.

Commonly Used Tools and Equipment

Most kitchens have the necessary equipment to prepare Tex-Mex dishes. Some special items may be used, but they are not required.

Griddle or Comal

A flat, smooth griddle is used in Mexican cooking to make tortillas.

Cooking Pan

Keep a variety on hand for cooking meats and sauces. To make tortillas, a flat-bottomed skillet can be used in place of a comal.

Grills

This will be useful when making fajitas and grilled tacos.

Knives Keep a variety of sharp knives on hand for slicing meat and vegetables.

Molcajete

Similar to a mortar and pestle, it is made of basalt. Used for grinding chillies and making masa or dough. To keep soups and other dishes warm, it is sometimes used as cookware and a serving dish.

Tortilla Press or Tortillero

When making tortillas, this is used to flatten the masa or dough.

Methods of Cooking

Meats are frequently cut into large pieces and grilled or fried (in contrast to traditional Mexican cuisine). Other cooking methods for vegetables and meats include boiling and stewing. Grilling on a barbecue or indoor grill is the most common method for searing meats and other ingredients.

Whether you're a novice or a seasoned chef, there's something here for you. With a better understanding of the history of Tex-Mex and its significance in American food culture and history, it's time to bring this comfort food into your kitchens!

SNACKS, APPETIZERS, AND DIPS

Dip with Queso

2-3 servings

Time to Prepare: 5 minutes

Time to cook: 10-15 minutes

Ingredients

1 litre evaporated milk

1 teaspoon corn starch

8

2 cups of your favourite shredded cheese (like cheddar or Gouda)

1 to 2 cups cream cheese or cream (optional)

1 tbsp. diced tomatoes with green chillies

½ pounds lean ground beef, cooked and drained

Directions

1. In a saucepan, combine the cornstarch and evaporated milk.
2. Stir in the shredded cheese and, if using, the cream cheese or cream.
3. Cook, stirring constantly, over medium heat until the cheese is melted, then continue cooking until the sauce is the desired thickness.
4. Stir in the cooked ground beef and the tomato-chilli mixture.
5. Cook until thoroughly heated.
6. Serve with tortilla chips or your favourite chips.

Guacamole Tex-Mex Style

3-4 servings

Time to Prepare: 10 minutes

Time to cook: 0 minutes

Ingredients

3 peeled and pitted ripe avocados

Lime juice (half a lime)

1 to 2 teaspoons salt, or to taste

2 tbsp. soured cream

10

12 tsp. olive oil (optional)

12 cup diced onion

2 diced small tomatoes

1 garlic clove, minced

3 tbsp fresh cilantro, to taste, chopped Cayenne or chilli pepper

To taste, cumin powder

Directions

1. Depending on your preference, the avocados can be prepared chunky or smooth.
2. In a mixing bowl, combine the mashed avocado, lime juice, salt, sour cream, and olive oil (optional, for extra smoothness).
3. Combine the onion, tomatoes, garlic, cilantro, cayenne or chilli pepper, and cumin powder in a mixing bowl (optional).
4. Can be eaten right away or prepared about 1 hour before serving (refrigerate); not too long before serving to avoid too much avocado discolouration.
5. Serve alongside tortilla chips, burritos, tacos, enchiladas, or tostadas.

Classic Tex-Mex Salsa

Time to prepare: 15 minutes plus 1 hour of refrigeration

Time to cook: 0 minutes

Ingredients

1 (10-ounce) can of diced tomatoes and green chillies

1 can (14 oz.) whole tomatoes, undrained

13 cup cilantro leaves

14 cup chopped onion

2 minced garlic cloves

14 teaspoon salt 1 jalapeno, thinly sliced, with or without seeds as desired

1 tbsp freshly squeezed lime juice

1 teaspoon ground cumin, or to taste

Adding sugar to taste (optional)

If desired, add chilli powder or hot sauce.

Directions

1. In a blender, combine all of the ingredients EXCEPT the chilli powder/hot sauce and pulse until smooth.
2. Chill for at least an hour before serving to allow flavours to develop.
3. If necessary, add more salt, lime, and sugar (to reduce heat) or hot sauce (to add heat) to taste.

Picnic at Pico de Gallo

Preparation Time: 15 minutes Servings: 2

Time to cook: 0 minutes

Ingredients

1 ½ cup seeded and finely diced tomatoes, preferably Roma

½ cup finely chopped cilantro

½ cup finely chopped white onion

1-2 small jalapeno peppers, finely chopped, seeded or not (depending on preference)

1-2 tablespoons lime juice, freshly squeezed

1 tablespoon finely chopped green onion (optional)

Season with salt to taste

Directions

1. If you are not using Roma tomatoes, drain the juice.
2. Mix all of the ingredients and serve.
3. Can be stored in the refrigerator for a day or two, but the flavour will change.
4. After storing, drain any liquid.

Servings of Bean & Cheese Nachos

Time to Prepare: 10 minutes

Time to cook: 11-16 minutes

Ingredients

36 tortilla chips made from corn (or 6 corn tortillas, each cut into 6 wedges)

Brushing with 1-2 tablespoons vegetable oil

1 pound of refried beans

1 cup shredded cheese of your choice (such as Gouda, cheddar, Monterey Jack, or Edam)

1/4 cup chopped cilantro (optional)

16

1 sliced jalapeno (optional)

1/2 cup salsa/pico de gallo

Directions.

1. Preheat the oven to 350 degrees Fahrenheit.
2. Arrange the tortillas on a baking sheet in a single layer.
3. If using corn tortillas, arrange them on a baking sheet in a single layer and brush lightly with oil. Bake for 10-15 minutes, or until crisp.
4. Pile refried beans and shredded cheese on top of the toasted tortilla chips.
5. Return to the oven and bake for 1 minute, or until the cheese is melted.
6. If desired, garnish with cilantro and jalapeno and serve with salsa or pico de gallo on the side.

Time to Prepare: 15 minutes

Time to cook: 20-25 minutes

Ingredients

2 russet potatoes, peeled (or unpeeled) and cut into 1-inch cubes

5 tablespoons olive oil divided in freshly boiled water to soak potatoes

1 teaspoon of salt for potatoes

1 tsp. garlic powder

1 diced onion

1 teaspoon of salt for the sauce

1 garlic clove, finely chopped

1 minced red chilli

½ tsp smoked paprika

1 can (14 oz.) whole peeled tomatoes, drained Cilantro, chopped, for garnish

1/4 cup mayonnaise

Directions

1. Soak the cubed potatoes for 10-15 minutes in freshly boiled, hot water.
2. Preheat the oven to 450 degrees Fahrenheit.
3. Drain and pat dry the soaked potatoes with paper towels.
1. Put them in a mixing bowl.
4. Toss in 3 tablespoons olive oil, salt, and garlic powder to coat.
5. Arrange the seasoned potatoes in a single layer on a baking sheet that has been lightly greased.
6. Bake until golden brown and cooked through, stirring halfway through (about 20 minutes). Prick the potatoes with a fork or toothpick to see if they are done. Place them in a serving dish.
7. Make the sauce while the potatoes are baking. In a large saucepan over medium heat, heat the remaining 2 tablespoons of olive oil.
8. Add the onion and 1 teaspoon salt, and cook until the onion softens and releases its juices (about 3 minutes).
2. Simmer for 2 minutes after adding the garlic, chilli, and paprika.

19

9. Stir in the tomatoes and return to low heat.
10. Pour the mixture into a blender, cover, and puree until smooth. Transfer to a mixing bowl.
11. Make a separate bowl for the mayonnaise.
12. Garnish baked potatoes with chopped cilantro and serve with dips of pureed tomato sauce and mayonnaise.

Servings of Chili Cheese Fries

Time to Prepare: 5 minutes

Time to cook: 30 minutes

Ingredients

1 bag of frozen French fries (28 oz.)

3–4 cups chili de Carne

20

3 cups shredded cheese of choice (for example, cheddar, Edam, Monterey, or Colby Jack)

Directions

1. Preheat the oven to 425 degrees Fahrenheit.

2. Arrange the French fries on a cookie sheet in a single layer.

3. Bake until the potatoes are partially cooked (about 15 minutes). Meanwhile, heat the chilli in a saucepan over medium heat until thoroughly heated.

4. Remove the fries from the oven and evenly distribute the heated chilli on top.

5. Sprinkle with cheese and return to the oven.

6. Bake for 10 minutes, or until the fries are done and the cheese is melted.

7. Plate and serve.

Toast from Texas

8 servings

Time to Prepare: 5 minutes

Time to cook: 15 minutes

Ingredients:

1-2 sticks of melted butter

1 teaspoon garlic powder

½ teaspoons of salt

1 teaspoon dried oregano

1 cup grated cheese (Monterey Jack, for example) Jack

1 baguette or loaf of bread, sliced into 1-inch slices

Chopped cilantro for garnish

Directions

1. Preheat the oven to 375 degrees Fahrenheit.
2. Combine the melted butter, garlic powder, salt, and oregano in a mixing bowl.
3. Brush the bread slices with the butter mixture.
4. Scatter the cheese over the bread and place it on a baking sheet.
5. Bake for 15 minutes, turning the pan halfway through, or until the cheese is melted and the bread is browned (about 15 minutes).
6. Garnish with chopped cilantro and serve while still hot.

Diablos de Shrimp

3 servings

Time to Prepare: 10 minutes

Time to cook: 8-10 minutes

Ingredients

12 jumbo raw shrimp (peeled and deveined)

2 medium jalapeno peppers, seeded and sliced into 12 long strips

23 cup white cheese, cut into 18-inch slices (such as queso fresco, dry ricotta, feta, or dry cottage cheese)

24

1 shallot, sliced 12 bacon slices

Directions

1. Preheat the oven to 425 degrees Fahrenheit.
2. Prepare a baking sheet by lining it with parchment paper.
3. Combine one shrimp with a slice of jalapeno, a slice of cheese, and a few slices of shallot. Wrap it in bacon and secure it with a toothpick. Rep with the remaining shrimp pieces.
4. Bake for 8-10 minutes, flipping the shrimp halfway through to brown on both sides.

SANDWICHES AND TORTILLA WRAPS

Tortillas from scratch

10-12 people

Time to prepare: 15 minutes plus 5 to 15 minutes of resting time

Time to cook: 15 minutes

Ingredients

3 cups all-purpose flour

2 teaspoons baking soda (optional)

1/4 cup olive oil (or lard)

3/4 cup ice-cold water

1 teaspoon sea salt

Extra flour is required for dusting while rolling and cooking.

Directions

1. In a mixing bowl, combine the flour, baking powder, oil, and water and knead lightly to form a dough. The dough should be soft and not stick to your fingers. To adjust the consistency, add a little more flour (if it's too gooey or sticky) or oil (if it's too stiff).
2. Shape into 10-12 balls and dust with flour to prevent them from drying out. Allow for 5-15 minutes of resting time, depending on how much the dough was kneaded.
3. Flatten and shape the dough into discs of the desired thickness and diameter with a rolling pin. To prevent sticking, dust with flour.
4. Cook the freshly rolled-out tortillas one at a time in a non-stick pan (about 30 seconds on each side).
5. To keep the cooked tortillas soft and pliable, cover them with a clean kitchen towel.
6. Place the cooked tortillas on a towel to cool. Cooled tortillas can be frozen in resealable bags for later use.
1. Although these can be frozen for several months, they do not taste as good as freshly made tortillas.
7. To heat the tortillas, wrap them in damp towels, 5 pieces at a time, and microwave for 20- 30 seconds. You can also heat them for 15 seconds on each side in a hot skillet.
8. It can be served hot or cold.

Burrito with Shredded Chicken

4 servings

Time to prepare: 15 minutes plus 1 hour of marinating time

Time to cook: 10 minutes

Ingredients

For the marinade

1/2 cups of water

1 tablespoon soy sauce

1 teaspoon sea salt

1 tablespoon brown sugar

1/2 tsp onion powder

1/4 tsp liquid smoke flavouring

1/4 tsp black pepper

1/4 tsp chilli powder

To fill

2 boneless skinless chicken breasts

1 cup rice, cooked

1 enchilada sauce (12 cups)

12 teaspoons of salt

4 flour tortillas (12 inches)

1/3 cup shredded cheese (such as Edam, cheddar, Monterey Jack, or a blend of the three combination)

2-3 tablespoons sliced green onion

Directions

1. Combine the marinade ingredients and marinate the 1-hour minimum marinating time for chicken (to overnight).
1. After marinating, grill the chicken until done over medium heat.
2. (Approximately 10-15 minutes, flipping halfway through grilling)

29

3. Shred the grilled chicken by slicing it thinly or pulling it apart. Set it up.
4. aside.
5. Combine the rice and enchilada sauce in a saucepan.
5. Season with salt and pepper. Cook, stirring constantly, until thoroughly heated.
6. Steam the tortillas by wrapping them in damp towels and placing them in a steaming pan.
6. Microwave on high for 20-30 seconds. You can also heat it. Cook them for 15 seconds on each side in a preheated skillet.
7. To assemble the burritos, start with 14 shredded chicken. in the middle of each tortilla
8. Spread a layer of rice over the chicken and top with cheese. Then garnish with green onions.
7. Fold one side of the tortilla over the other to wrap the burritos. Pull back to cover the filling in half. Apply pressure to the edges. to compact the filling and achieve a tight roll Fold one of the ends over to Seal and roll the burrito to the end. Both ends could be
8. If desired, seal the container.
9. Microwave the burrito for a few seconds to warm it up. simply to melt the cheese

Burrito with Beans

8 servings

Time to Prepare: 15 minutes

Time to cook: 30-35 minutes

Ingredients

2 teaspoons olive oil

2 medium chopped onions

4 chopped garlic cloves

1 seeded and chopped jalapeno chilli

½ teaspoon cumin powder

seasoned with salt and pepper

three tbsp tomato paste

3 cans (15 oz.) of pinto beans, drained and rinsed

12 cup water

1 box (10 oz.) of frozen corn kernels

12 cups thinly sliced green onions

8 flour tortillas (10 inches)

1 cup rice, cooked

2 cups shredded cheese (such as Edam, cheddar, Monterey Jack, or a blend of the three

combination)

Sour cream, salsa, and guacamole (optional)

Directions

1. In a large saucepan over medium heat, heat the oil.

2. Season with cumin and add the onions, garlic, and jalapeno. seasoned with salt and pepper Cook until browned (about 10-12 minutes).

3. Cook for 1 minute after adding the tomato paste.

4. Bring the beans and water to a boil in a saucepan.

5. Reduce the heat to low and continue to cook, stirring occasionally, until

increased in thickness (about 10-12 minutes).

6. Cook for 2 to 3 minutes after adding the corn.

7. Remove from heat and top with green onions. Wrap the tortillas in damp towels and steam them for 8 minutes. Microwave on high for 20-30 seconds. You can also heat it. Cook them for 15 seconds on each side in a preheated skillet.

9. To assemble the burrito, layer 18 portions of the beans, rice, and cheese in the middle of a warmed tortilla

10. Fold one side of the tortilla over the other and pull it back to form a triangle. encase the filling To pack the filling, press down on the edges to achieve a tight roll Seal one end by folding it over and rolling the whole thing up burrito all the way. If desired, both ends can be sealed.

11. Place the burrito on a baking sheet, seam side down, and bake for 15 minutes. Make the rest of the burritos.

12. Bake for 20-30 minutes at 425°F, or until crisp and heated through.

13. Burritos can be wrapped in plastic wrap and frozen for up to 3 months up to three months Defrost in the microwave OR wrap in foil and place in the refrigerator. Preheat the oven to 425°F and bake for 40-50 minutes. Remove the tortillas from the oven to make crisp burritos. During the last 10 minutes of baking, cover with foil.

14. Serve immediately with salsa, guacamole, and sour cream, if desired.

The Chimichanga (Deep Fried Burrito)

4 servings

Time to prepare: 20 minutes

Time to cook: 35-40 minutes

Ingredients

4 flour tortillas, large

2 cups vegetable oil (for frying)

To fill
34

1 pound of meat of your choice (chicken or beef)

1 chopped small onion

1 medium destemmed, seeded, and chopped bell pepper

3 Roma tomatoes, diced

1 minced garlic clove Season with salt and pepper to taste.

½ cup refried beans

½ cup salsa, guacamole, and sour cream, plus extra for garnish serving

Directions

1. Combine the meat, onion, bell pepper, tomatoes, salt, and pepper in a mixing bowl pepper in a heavy-bottomed pot, thoroughly mixing to coat the meat.
2. Cook for 45 minutes over medium heat, covered. Stir occasionally.
3. Remove from the heat and set aside to cool.
4. Once the meat has cooled, shred it by pulling it apart with forks, or thinly slice it with a sharp knife Return the meat to the pan. Set it aside with the vegetables.
5. In a saucepan over medium heat, heat the refried beans until they are warm heated through and through (about 5 minutes).
6. Steam the tortillas by wrapping them in damp towels and placing them in a steaming pan. Microwave on high for 20-30 seconds. You can also heat it. Cook them for 15 seconds on each side in a preheated skillet.
7. Place 14 of the warmed refried beans in the centre of each tortilla.

8. Arrange 14 of the shredded meat on top of the refried beans.

9. Serve with spoonsful of salsa, guacamole, and sour cream. Meat and refried beans

10. Fold over one side of the tortilla. While exerting pressure Fold the sides in to seal the ends around the middle. Continue to turn the tortilla over so that the centre is resting on the opposite end of a tortilla Place seam side down on a tray or dish. Repeat for the remainder of the tortillas

11. In a frying pan over medium-high heat, heat the oil.

12. Fry the chimichangas for 5 minutes, or until lightly browned and crisp on both sides).

13. Using a slotted spoon, remove the fried chaturangas from the oil and pat them dry with paper towels for a few seconds.

14. Serve immediately with additional salsa, guacamole, and sour cream.

Beef Quesadilla

4 servings

Time to prepare: 20 minutes

Time to cook: 10 minutes

Ingredients

1-pound minced beef

½ cup refried beans

1 can (4 oz.) chopped green chillies, drained

½ tsp dried oregano

½ teaspoon cumin powder

½ teaspoon salt 1 teaspoon chilli powder or to taste

4 flour tortillas (8 inches)

2 tbsp. melted butter or margarine

1 1/3 cups shredded cheese of your choice

Paprika

Directions

1. In a skillet over medium heat, brown the beef until it is no longer pink (5-10 minutes). Remove any excess liquid.
2. Combine the beans, chillies, oregano, cumin, chilli powder, and salt in a mixing bowl.

37

3. Stir in the remaining ingredients and reduce the heat to medium-low. Cook until thoroughly heated (about 3-4 minutes). Allow cooling after removing from the heat.
4. Preheat the oven to 475 degrees Fahrenheit. Spread butter on one side of each tortilla.
5. Spread 12 cups of the meat mixture on half of a tortilla's unbuttered side.
6. Top with 13 cups cheese and fold in half. Place on a baking sheet that has been lightly greased.
7. Bake until crisp and golden brown, then sprinkle with paprika (about 10 minutes).
8. Slice into wedges and serve.

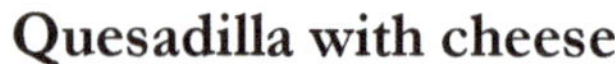

Quesadilla with cheese

4 servings

Time to Prepare: 5 minutes

Time to cook: 16 minutes

Ingredients

4 flour tortillas (10 inches)

1 cup shredded cheese of choice

4 tablespoons melted butter

Sour cream, salsa, and guacamole

Directions

1. Spread 14 cups of cheese over half of a tortilla, leaving space in between the rims.
2. Fold the tortilla in half to form a half-moon.
3. In a heavy skillet over low heat, melt 1 tablespoon of butter.
4. Cook one half-moon tortilla in the skillet until browned on only one side (about 2 minutes). Brown the other side carefully as well as the other side Place in a serving dish. Rep for each the remaining tortillas. Garnish with salsa, guacamole, and sour cream.

4 servings

Time to Prepare: 10 minutes

Time to cook: 15 minutes

Ingredients

frying oil

To make dough

2 cups harina (masa harina) (Mexican corn flour)

1 tsp. baking powder

12 teaspoons of salt

1 Tbsp. vegetable oil

1/4 cups of hot water (approximately)

To fill

shredded or cooked meat (chicken, beef, pork, chorizo, bacon, etc.)

chopped

Beans refried

Choice of cheese and shredded lettuce

Onion, jalapeno, tomato, avocado, and cilantro, sliced

Sour cream, salsa, guacamole, pico de gallo, and guacamole

Directions

Making the gordita pockets

1. In a mixing bowl, combine the masa harina, baking powder, and salt.bowl.
2. Pour in about a cup of water and the oil. Incorporate and gradually. Add the remaining water just enough to make a dough that sticks together to form a ball It should not cling to

your hands. a small amount. If it becomes too sticky, add more flour.

3   Separate the dough into four equal pieces and pat or roll each one out to a 4-5-inch-wide circle with a 12-inch thickness.
4   4.Heat the oil in a 1-inch-deep pan to 360-375°F. You can Drop a tiny piece of dough into the oil to test it. If it floats to the surface, the oil is ready when it sizzles.
5   Place the gorditas in the hot oil and cook until they rise to the surface (about 2 minutes). Fry for another 30 minutes on the other side seconds. Drain on absorbent paper after removing from the oil. Allow them to cool.
6   To include filling
7   Make a pocket on the side of the cooled gordita.
8   Stuff with your preferred fillings and serve.

Chalupas

5 people

Time to Prepare: 10 minutes

Time to cook: 10 minutes

Ingredients

5 tortillas (corn or flour)

2 quarts of cooking oil

To fill

Cooked meat (such as chicken, beef, or pork), shredded or cubed

Beans refried

Choice of cheese and shredded lettuce

Onion, jalapeno, tomato, avocado, and cilantro, sliced

Sour cream, salsa, guacamole, pico de gallo, and guacamole

Directions

1. Arrange the fillings so that they are ready while the chalupas are still warm.

   <u>Making chalupas</u>

43

2. If you're making your dough, roll out uncooked dough. Apply additional pressure to the centre of the tortilla circle. Alternatively, a disc can be used to thin out the centre. This will make folding easier later frying.

3. Preheat the oil in a skillet to 350°F. Drop a teeny-tiny piece of In the hot oil, place the dough. It should sizzle and float to the top of the water.

4. It will take about 1 hour to fry the tortillas until they are golden brown each for one-minute Fry the tortillas as if they were in a boat. with a pair of tongs, shape If you're making your dough, You can fold them after frying if the centres have been thinned. They're still hot.

To include filling

5. Stuff the chalupas with the desired filling and serve.

Santa Fe Wrap

serves 4 people.

Time to prepare: 20 minutes

Time to cook: 10 minutes

Ingredients

4 flour tortillas (10 inches), cooked Santa Fe cream

1 cup softened cream cheese

1-2 tablespoons lime juice

1 teaspoon dried oregano

1-2 minced garlic cloves

½ teaspoon chopped cilantro

8 ounces extra-lean ground beef

<u>for filling</u>

1 cup rinsed and drained canned black beans

1 pound chunky salsa

2 tablespoons sliced green onions

½ cup shredded cheese (such as Edam, cheddar, Monterey Jack, or a combination of these)

½ cup lettuce, shredded

½ cup diced tomato

4 tablespoons Santa Fe ice cream

The sour cream (optional)

Directions

1. Brown the ground beef in a skillet over medium heat.
2. Remove any excess fat and add the beans. Cook, stirring gently, until thoroughly heated.
3. Remove the pan from the heat and set it aside to cool for a few minutes.

4. Divide the mixture into four equal portions and spoon one into each tortilla.
5. Separate the remaining ingredients and arrange them down the centre of the tortillas.
6. Roll up like a burrito.

Bocadito (Tea Sandwich)

8 servings

Time to prepare: 20 minutes

Time to cook: 0 minutes

Ingredients

8-12 sweet rolls or 1 loaf of thinly sliced white bread, crust removed

Regarding the spread

1 (8 oz.) package of cream cheese

4 tbsp of mayonnaise

12 cup chopped pimento-stuffed olives

12 cup chopped ham (or cooked tuna or salmon flakes, if desired)

(chicken shredded)

As a garnish (optional)

a little more cream cheese

Cooked ham, tuna, salmon, and other seafood slices

thinly sliced olives, cucumber, or tomatoes; lime zest or chopped

cilantro

Directions

1. Combine the cream cheese and mayonnaise until smooth.

2. Combine the ham and pimientos in a mixing bowl.

48

3. Spread a slice of bread with some of the mixtures. Finish with a cut a second slice of bread into small finger sandwiches of

your preferred shape Garnish with your preferred garnish.

(optional).

4. You can also make open sandwiches with the spread piped on top.

top (chill the spread first), then garnishes

Enchiladas

4 servings

Time to Prepare: 15 minutes

Time to cook: 20 minutes

Ingredients

Sauce for enchiladas

(approximately 4 cups)

1/4 cup melted coconut oil, canola oil, or vegetable oil

1/4 cup unbleached all-purpose flour

50

three tbsp chilli powder

1 cup chicken broth

1 can of crushed tomatoes (28 oz.)

1 tsp. dried oregano

1 tablespoon cumin

1 tsp. garlic powder

1 tsp onions powder

1 tbsp brown sugar packed

1/2 tsp kosher salt

1 teaspoon black pepper, ground

<u>To assemble the enchiladas</u>

4 tortillas (corn or flour)

4 chicken breast fillets OR 1 13 cups cooked shredded chicken

(You can make vegetarian enchiladas with a combination of cooked vegetables and tofu.)

(For example, black beans, cauliflower, spinach, broccoli, and so on.)

2 cups shredded cheese (Edam, cheddar, Monterey Jack, or a combination of the three)

combination), separated

51

13 cup finely chopped onion

1-pound enchilada sauce

Chopped cilantro for garnish (optional)

Guacamole and sour cream

Directions

<u>To make enchilada sauce</u>

1. In a medium saucepan over medium heat, combine the oil and flour heat. Combine the remaining ingredients in a mixing bowl. Adjust the seasoning to taste. spices based on your tastes
2. Place any unused enchilada sauce in an airtight container and set aside.

   It can be stored in the refrigerator for up to two weeks.

<u>To assemble the enchiladas</u>

3. Preheat the oven to 350 degrees Fahrenheit.
4. Grease a 2-quart baking dish with cooking spray and pour in about 12 cups of Incorporate enchilada sauce into it. Set it aside for now.
5. Combine the shredded chicken (or vegetable mixture) in a mixing bowl. In a mixing bowl, combine your choice of cheese, 1 cup of cheese, and the onion. Set it aside for now.
6. Steam the tortillas by wrapping them in damp towels and placing them in a steaming pan. Microwave on high for 20-30 seconds. You can also heat it. Cook them for 15 seconds on each side in a preheated skillet. This is to soften the tortillas.
7. Arrange a warmed tortilla in the baking dish with the enchilada. sauce (This can also be done on a separate surface if necessary.)

It's too muddled). Place some of the chicken/vegetable filling on top.

1. Roll the tortilla to form a cylinder in the centre. Put it there. seam side down, against the edge of the baking dish Carryout the same with the remaining tortillas, neatly lining and packing the rolls in the baking pan.

8. Spoon the remaining enchilada sauce over the rolls (adding more if desired). sauce, if using) and top with the remaining cheese.

9. Cover with foil and bake for 15 minutes, or until heated through minutes.

10. Remove the foil and bake for another 5 minutes to melt the chocolate cheese.

11. Garnish with cilantro (optional) and serve with sour cream. Guacamole and cream.

Flanges (Fried Tortilla Rolls)

6 people

Time to Prepare: 25 minutes

Time to cook: 35 minutes

Ingredients

1 package (10 oz.) of corn tortillas

1-quart salsa

2 cups frying vegetable oil

To fill

1 tablespoon of vegetable oil

1/2 seeded and chopped green bell pepper

1/2 finely diced onion

1-pound boneless, skinless chicken breast, cut into 1-inch chunks (ground beef or pork may also be used)

1 1/2 teaspoon chilli powder, or 14 teaspoon garlic powder, to taste

1/4 teaspoon red pepper flakes, crushed

1/4 tsp dried oregano

1/2 tsp. paprika

1 teaspoon cumin powder

1 teaspoon kosher salt

3/4 cups of water

12 cup shredded cheese (Edam, cheddar, Monterey Jack, etc.)

Directions

<u>To prepare the filling</u>

1. In a skillet over medium heat, heat the oil.
2. Saute the bell pepper and onion until the onion is softened (about 5 minutes).
3. Turn the heat up to medium-high and add the chicken breast or ground meat.
4. Cook, stirring constantly until the meat is no longer pink in the centre (about 10 minutes).
5. Shred the chicken breasts with two forks if used.
6. Combine the seasonings and spices with the water in a mixing bowl.
7. Simmer, stirring occasionally, until the liquid has evaporated (about 10 minutes).
8. Remove from the heat and set aside after stirring in the cheese. To prepare the flats
9. Lightly brush each corn tortilla with salsa.
10. Spread about 2 tablespoons of the filling along the bottom edge of the tortilla, then tightly roll it into a cylinder and secure the ends with one or two toothpicks. Repeat with the rest of the tortillas.
11. In a large skillet, heat 2 cups of vegetable oil to 375°F.
12. Fry the flautas in the preheated oil for 4 minutes, or until golden and crisp. Don't fry too many at once.
13. Drain on absorbent paper or paper towels.

55

14. Take out the toothpicks.
15. Serve with additional salsa on the side.

RICE, SALADS AND BOWLS

Tex-Mex Chili Bowl

4 servings

Time to Prepare: 15 minutes

Time to cook: 55-60 minutes

Ingredients

4 cups cooked long-grain rice

1-quart sour cream

<u>Chipotle con Carne</u>

1 tbsp vegetable or cooking oil

1 large minced onion

1 seeded and chopped red pepper

2 garlic cloves, peeled and minced

1–3 teaspoons chilli powder, to taste

1 tablespoon paprika

1 teaspoon cumin powder

1-pound minced lean beef, cut into small cubes

1/4 cup beef broth

1 can of chopped tomatoes (14 oz.)

two tbsp tomato paste

12 tsp dried marjoram

1 teaspoon granulated sugar

Season with salt and pepper to taste.

1 can (14 oz.) rinsed and drained red kidney beans

Directions

1. Heat the oil in a medium-sized, heavy-bottomed pot over medium heat.
2. Add the onion and cook until it is tender (about 5 minutes).
3. Combine the red pepper, garlic, chilli powder, paprika, and cumin in a mixing bowl.
4. Continue to cook for another 5 minutes.
5. Turn up the heat to high and add the beef.
6. Stir to evenly brown the beef. Cook it until it is well browned (about 5 minutes). Remove any excess grease.
7. Combine the beef stock, chopped tomatoes, tomato paste, marjoram, sugar, salt, and pepper in a mixing bowl.
8. Stir thoroughly and bring to a boil.
9. Cover and turn down the heat. Allow for a 20-minute simmer, stirring occasionally. If the sauce begins to dry out, add a tablespoon of water at a time to achieve the desired consistency. The sauce should be thick but not too thick.
10. Stir in the kidney beans, which have been drained. Bring it to a boil by increasing the heat. Reduce the heat to low and leave to simmer (uncovered) for 10 minutes. If necessary, add more water to prevent the bottom from drying out or scorching.
11. To taste, add more seasonings to enhance the flavour.
12. Remove from the heat and cover with a lid. Allow the pot to sit for 10 minutes.
13. Serve with rice and sour cream on the side.

Salad with Tex-Mex Chicken

4 servings

Time to Prepare: 15 minutes

Time to cook: 0 minutes

Ingredients

12 cup chopped romaine lettuce and watercress

12 cup cilantro leaves 14 thinly sliced sweet onion

3 cups shredded skinless rotisserie chicken breast
60

2 cups peeled and chopped jicama

14 cup halved, seeded, and thinly sliced red jalapeno pepper

12 cup crumbled Cotija or feta cheese (Parmesan or Romana also work)

4 warmed flour tortillas

1 lime, peeled and cut into wedges

<u>To make salad dressing</u>

1/2 cup cilantro sprigs

1/2 cup Cotija or feta cheese, crumbled

1-quart buttermilk

1 lime juice, plus wedges for serving

1/4 halved, seeded, and thinly sliced red jalapeno pepper

season with salt to taste

Directions

1. To begin, make the dressing by combining all of the ingredients in a blender and pureeing them. Allow it to sit for at least 5 minutes to allow the flavours to meld.
2. In a large mixing bowl, combine the salad greens, cilantro, and half of the dressing.
3. Arrange the greens on a plate and top with the onion, chicken, jicama, and jalapenos.

61

1. Toss gently.
4. Top with the remaining dressing and sprinkle with cheese.
5. Serve with tortillas and wedges of lime.

Avocado Chicken Bowl

Serves 3 people

Time to Prepare: 15 minutes

Time to cook: 45-50 minutes

Ingredients

For the marinade

2 minced chipotle chillies in adobo sauce

2 teaspoons olive oil

2 tbsp freshly squeezed lime juice

1 tbsp chilli powder (or to taste)

3 minced garlic cloves

1 teaspoon cumin powder, or to taste

1 tsp kosher salt (or sea salt)

to taste, black pepper

3 halved boneless, skinless chicken breasts

Regarding rice

1 finely chopped red onion

12 cup white long-grain rice

3 cup chicken stock

12 tsp kosher salt

14 cups finely chopped fresh cilantro

2 tbsp freshly squeezed lime juice

1 (15 oz.) can be rinsed and drained with pinto or black beans

1 cup queso fresco or feta crumbles

2 wedged limes

2 peeled and diced avocados

three flour tortillas

Guacamole

Directions

1. To reduce the bite of the onions, rinse them with cold water. Drain and set aside to dry.
2. Combine the marinade ingredients. Fill a resealable bag or shallow container with a lid with the chicken. Seal the container after adding the marinade. Allow it to marinate in the refrigerator while you prepare the rest of the ingredients.
3. In a saucepan or pot, combine the rice, broth, and salt and bring to a simmer.
4. Turn down the heat to low. Cook, covered until the rice has absorbed all of the liquid (about 20 minutes). Preheat your grill to 350°F at this point.
5. Return to the rice, turn off the heat, and cover the pot for 10 minutes.
6. Add the cilantro and lime juice after ten minutes. Replace the lid on the pot and set it aside.
7. Remove the chicken from the marinade and grill it for about 10 minutes, lid down. Halfway through, flip it over. When there is no longer any pink in the centre of the chicken, it is done. Make sure not to charge the surface.
8. Remove the meat from the grill and set aside for 5 minutes to cool. It should be cut into bite-sized pieces.

9.   Ladle the rice into serving bowls.
10. Add chicken, onion, beans, and cheese to the top.
11. Garnish with lime wedges, diced avocado, tortilla chips, and guacamole if desired.

Classic Mexican rice

4-6 servings

Time to Prepare: 15 minutes

Time to cook: 40 minutes

Ingredients

1 13 cup very ripe fresh or canned tomatoes, cored

13 cup canola or other cooking oil 1 medium white onion, chopped

2 cups white long-grain rice

4 minced garlic cloves

2 medium seeded and minced jalapenos

2 c. chicken stock

1 teaspoon tomato paste

1/12 teaspoon salt

12 cup minced fresh cilantro

1 jalapeno, minced (seeded) for garnish

1 lime, peeled and cut into wedges

Directions

1. In a blender, combine the tomatoes and onion to make a smooth puree. Set it aside for now.
2. Place the rice in a strainer and rinse under cold running water until the starch has been removed and the water is clear. Drain \swell.

66

3. In a heavy-bottomed skillet, heat the oil over medium-low heat for about 2 minutes. When a grain of rice is dropped into the oil, it sizzles, and the oil is ready.
4. Sauté the rice in the oil for 6-8 minutes, or until it is light gold.
5. Saute the garlic and 2 minced seedless jalapenos until fragrant (about 1 minute).
6. Transfer the skillet contents to a rice cooker. Rinse any remaining bits from the skillet in the rice cooker with the broth.
1. Combine the puree, tomato paste, and salt in a mixing bowl.
7. Cover the rice cooker and leave it to cook for about 30 minutes. Remove from the heat but leave the lid on for another 5 minutes to ensure that the rice has absorbed all of the moisture.
8. Garnish with cilantro and jalapeno slices, and serve with lime wedges on the side.

Chicken, Rice and Pinto Beans Bowl

4-6 people

Time to prepare: 10 minutes plus 8 hours marinating

Time to cook: 40-60 minutes

Ingredients

1 halved chicken

a single recipe Rice from Mexico

4-6 pieces of warmed flour tortillas

Pico de gallo or chunky salsa,

For garnish, use shredded cheese.

Avocado slices (optional)

<u>To make the marinade</u>

1/4 cup cooking oil

1/4 cup melted butter

1/2 tsp onion powder

1/2 tsp garlic powder

1/4 teaspoon cumin powder

2 tsp lime or lemon juice

seasoned with salt and pepper

<u>To make the pinto beans</u>

1 Tbsp. vegetable oil

1 serrano chilli, whole

14 teaspoon ground chilli (like serrano, ancho or chipotle)

1 can of pinto beans (28 oz.)

13 cups of water

1 thinly sliced green onion

Directions

1. Combine the marinade ingredients and marinate the chicken for at least 8 hours in the refrigerator, covered.
2. Preheat the grill to medium-high after marinating the chicken.
3. Cook the chicken on the grill until it is evenly browned and cooked through (about 25 minutes).
4. Allow the meat to cool for about 5 minutes before cutting it into bite-sized pieces.
5. Heat the oil in a saucepan with the serrano chilli to prepare the pinto beans. Cook the chilli until it is tender. Combine the ground chillies, beans, and water in a mixing bowl. Bring it to a boil, stirring constantly. Reduce the heat to low and continue to cook for 15 minutes.
6. Ladle rice into bowls, then top with beans and chicken.
7. Garnish with shredded cheese and serve with tortillas and salsa or pico de gallo.

69

Vegetarian Tex-Mex Rice Bowl

4 servings

Time to Prepare: 15 minutes

Time to cook: 30-35 minutes

Ingredients

13 cup drained diced tomatoes

14 cups cooked and drained black beans

14 cups drained cooked whole kernel corn

1 sliced avocado

For garnish, use shredded cheese.

4 teaspoons chopped red onion

For garnish, use chopped fresh cilantro.

black pepper, freshly ground

wedges of lime

<u>Regarding rice</u>

2 cups broth (vegetable or chicken)

1 cup of water

1 tablespoon of olive oil

2 tbsp lime juice (divided)

1 cup short-grain brown rice, uncooked

14 cup chopped cilantro

1 cup chopped arugula

Season with salt and pepper to taste.

Directions

1. In a rice cooker, combine the chicken broth, water, olive oil, 1
   tablespoon lime juice, and rice and set it to cook.

71

1. When all of the water has been absorbed (about 20 minutes),
    remove from the heat and set aside for 5-10 minutes, covered.
2. Combine the cilantro, remaining lime juice, arugula, salt, and
    pepper in a mixing bowl.
3. Divide the rice among four bowls.
4. Arrange tomatoes, black beans, corn, and avocado slices on
    top of each bowl.
5. Sprinkle with cheese, onion, cilantro, and freshly ground black
    pepper to serve.
6. Garnish with lime wedges.

SOUPS

Mexican Beef Soup

6 people

Time to Prepare: 25 minutes

1 hour 15 minutes to cook

Ingredients

5 pounds stew beef bones (lean beef can be added or substituted)

4 minced garlic cloves

2 minced onions

season with salt to taste

4 husked ears of corn, cut in half 4 large peeled and cut into large chunks

3 peeled and cut carrots into 1-inch pieces

1 cup plantain bananas, thickly sliced if available (or use zucchini)

If available, 1 chayote, peeled, pitted, and cut into chunks

12 head cabbage, cut into 1 12" cubes

1 green bell pepper, seeded and sliced into 1-inch cubes

To taste, chilli powder

6 cups hot cooked rice

For garnish, use chopped fresh cilantro wedges of lime

Directions

1. Place any bones and meat in a stockpot.

2. Pour in enough water to cover by 6 inches, then bring to a boil.
3 Remove any scum.
4 Reduce the heat to low and continue to cook for 45 minutes.
5 Stir in the garlic, onion, and salt to taste.
6 Continue to boil for 15 minutes after adding the corn and potatoes.
7 Add the carrot, plantains, and chayote and mix well. Cook for an additional 10 minutes.
8 Cook for 5 minutes more after adding the cabbage and bell pepper.
9 Season with chilli powder to taste and remove from heat.
10 Ladle the soup into 6 large bowls and top each with 1 cup of hot rice.
11 Garnish with chopped cilantro and serve hot with lime wedges.

Tortilla Soup

Serves 4 people.

Time to Prepare: 15 minutes

Time to cook: 15 minutes

Ingredients

3 ears of corn

1 split and seeded red bell pepper

2 tablespoons olive oil

1-pound diced chicken breast tenders

1 tsp chicken seasoning

1 teaspoon cumin powder

seasoned with salt and pepper

1 medium or small zucchini, diced

1 medium chopped onion

3 garlic cloves, chopped

1-2 chopped chipotle peppers in adobo sauce

1 can stewed tomatoes (28 oz.)

1 can (8 oz.) tomato sauce

3 cup chicken broth

4 cups large-sized corn tortilla chips

1 ripe avocado, diced, dressed with 12 lemon juice

1/4 chopped red onion for garnish

Chopped cilantro for garnish

1 cup grated cheese (cheddar or Edam)

1/2 cup soured cream

Directions

1. Preheat the grill to medium-high heat.
2. Brush the corn and bell pepper with oil and grill for 10 minutes, turning halfway through.
3. Allow the vegetables to cool before removing any charred skin from the bell pepper. Remove the corn kernels from the cob and chop the bell pepper. Set these aside for now.
4. Meanwhile, in a soup pot, heat the oil and add the diced chicken.
5. Add poultry seasoning, cumin, salt, and pepper to taste. Cook until the chicken is lightly browned.
6. Combine the zucchini, onions, garlic, and chipotle peppers in a mixing bowl.
7. Continue to cook until the vegetables are softened (about 5 to 7 minutes).
8. Stir in the tomatoes, tomato sauce, and stock. Bring the water to a boil.
9. Reduce the heat to low heat and bring the soup to a simmer.

10. Stir in the corn kernels and bell pepper, and season with salt and pepper to taste.
11. Take the pan off the heat.
12. Ladle the soup into bowls and top with a handful of tortilla chips.
13. Serve with avocado, onion, cilantro, and shredded cheese as garnish.
    Serve with sour cream on top.

Soup with Tex-Mex Chicken

8 servings

Time to prepare: 20 minutes

Time to cook: 1 hour 50 minutes

Ingredients

5 pounds of chicken leg quarters (or soup bones combined with other parts)

3 tbsp. peeled and crushed garlic

2 teaspoons salt

2 bouillon cubes (chicken)

4 large peeled and cut carrots

4 large peeled and cut into large chunks of potatoes

4 large zucchini, cut into chunks

1 peeled and cut into large chunks chayote

1 large white onion, peeled and cut into large chunks

12 bunch chopped fresh cilantro

Directions

1. Place the chicken in a large pot and cover with water by 6 inches. Bring the water to a boil.
2. Stir in the garlic and salt. Simmer, covered, over low heat until the chicken meat falls off the bones (about 1 to 2 hours).
3. In a small bowl, dissolve the bouillon cubes in the broth.
4. Stir in the carrots, potatoes, zucchini, chayote, and white onion, and reduce the heat to medium-low.
5. Bring the soup to a low boil and cook until the carrots and potatoes are tender (about 45 minutes).

6. Add the chopped cilantro to the soup and simmer for 5
   minutes before serving.

TACOS

Basic Taco Shell

20-24 people

Time to Prepare: 5 minutes

Time to cook: 10-12 minutes

Ingredients:

homemade flour tortillas or store-bought tortillas

Directions

1. Make the flour tortillas according to the recipe.

81

2. To soften store-bought or cold tortillas, wrap 5 pieces in a damp towel and microwave for 25-30 seconds.
3. Preheat the oven to 375 degrees Fahrenheit.
4. Drape the tortillas over the grill rack in the oven. The ends should hang through the slots, while the middle section should rest on about two grill bars. The tortillas will then be baked in the shape of a taco.
5. Bake for 8-10 minutes, or until the top is crisp.
6. Heat 1 inch of oil to 375°F for frying. Slide a tortilla in carefully and cook for 15 seconds. Fold it in half with a pair of tongs and fry it "open" for 15 seconds more before draining on absorbent paper. While it's still hot, season with salt.

Tacos de Carne

10 servings

Time to Prepare: 15 minutes

Time to cook: 15 minutes

Ingredients

1-pound lean ground beef (ground pork or sliced chicken can be substituted)

1 cup salsa chunky

Taco shells (10)

12 head shredded lettuce

1 medium chopped tomato or 1 cup pico de gallo

12 cup minced onion

1 cup cheddar cheese, shredded

The sour cream (optional)

Directions

1. In a skillet over medium heat, brown the beef for about 10 minutes, breaking up any lumps with a spatula. Remove any excess oil.
2. Add the salsa and bring to a boil.
3. Reduce the heat to low and continue to cook the mixture for 5 minutes.
1. Place it in a bowl.
4. Warm the taco shells in the oven for 5 minutes, as directed on the package, or in the microwave for 45 seconds.
5. Assemble the tacos with beef, lettuce, tomato or pico de gallo, onion, and shredded cheese. Serve with sour cream on top.

Tacos de Veggies

10 servings

Time to Prepare: 15 minutes

Time to cook: 3-5 minutes

Ingredients

1 pound of refried beans

Taco shells (10)

1 cup salsa chunky

3 peeled, pitted, and sliced avocados

12 cup minced onion

Shredded lettuce, chopped tomatoes, pico de gallo, chopped cilantro, sour cream, and chopped green onion are among the additional toppings.

Directions

1. Put the refried beans in a microwave-safe bowl. Cover and heat until hot, stirring occasionally with a wooden spoon.
2. Warm the taco shells in the oven for 5 minutes, as directed on the package, or in the microwave for 45 seconds.
3. Add refried beans and/or avocado to the taco shells.
4. Toss in the salsa, onion, and other desired toppings.

Tacos de Pork Tex-Mex

6 people

Time to prepare: 20 minutes plus 30 minutes of soaking time

Time to cook: 2 hours 40 minutes

Ingredients

a total of 24 6-inch corn or wheat tortillas

4 trimmed and thinly sliced radishes

Onions, chopped for salsa

Onions pickled

chopped cilantro

<u>To make a pork shoulder</u>

4 large stemmed and seeded dried ancho chillies

2 large dried árbol chillies, stemmed and seeded

2 teaspoons sugar

1 tablespoon freshly squeezed lime juice

1 boneless pork shoulder (approximately 5 pounds)

Kosher salt or sea salt

two tbsp vegetable oil

1 large chopped onion

4 cloves garlic, coarsely chopped

two bay leaves

2 teaspoons oregano (dried)

2 teaspoons coriander powder

2 teaspoons cumin powder

12 tsp ground allspice

1 bottle (12 oz.) dark beer

Directions

1. Soak the dried chillies for 30 minutes in hot, freshly boiled water. Cover them with a plate or saucer and weigh them down. 1 cup of liquid should be saved after draining.
2. Preheat the oven to 350 degrees Fahrenheit.
3. Make a paste with the chillies, sugar, lime juice, and 14 cups of the reserved soaking liquid in a blender. If necessary, add more soaking liquid.
4. Using paper towels, pat dries the pork shoulder.
5. Season liberally with salt, then rub the paste evenly over the pork.
6. In a large Dutch oven or heavy pot, heat the oil over medium heat. Cook until the onion, garlic, bay leaves, oregano, coriander, cumin, and allspice are tender (about 8 minutes).
7. Add the beer and bring it to a boil.
8. Put the pork in the pot, cover it, and place it in the oven. Allow it to braise for about 2 12 hours, basting occasionally with pan juices.
9. When the pork is done, carefully transfer it to a large tray and set it aside to cool.
10. Shred the meat with forks and pour the pan juice over it.

In a skillet, heat the tortillas for about 1 minute on each side, then wrap them in towels to keep them warm.

11. Serve warm tacos and shredded pork with a variety of toppings on the side for everyone to use as they please.

Tacos de Carne Asada (Grilled Marinated Beef)

Serves 8

Time to prepare: 1 hour to overnight marinating

Time to cook: 15-20 minutes

Ingredients

3 lbs flank steaks

2 teaspoons olive oil

8 tortillas (corn or flour)

12 cup salsa

2 cups Cotija or feta cheese, grated

wedges of lime

To make the marinade

13 cup distilled white vinegar

12 c. soy sauce

4 minced garlic cloves

2 limes juice

12 cup extra-virgin olive oil

1 teaspoon sea salt

1 teaspoon black pepper, ground

1 teaspoon ground white pepper

1 tsp. garlic powder

1 tablespoon chilli powder

1 tsp. dried oregano

1 teaspoon cumin powder

1 tablespoon paprika

To make the onion relish

12 cups chopped fresh cilantro 1 white onion, chopped

One lime juice

Directions

1. Combine the marinade ingredients and pour over the flank steak. Allow it to marinate for 1 hour overnight.
2. Make the onion relish by combining all of the ingredients in a mixing bowl.
1. Set it aside for now.
2. Cut the flank steak into small cubes or strips after marinating.
3. Heat the oil in a medium skillet over medium heat, and cook the meat strips, stirring constantly, until the liquid has evaporated. Set aside after removing from the heat.
4. To heat the tortillas, wrap them in damp towels, 5 at a time, and microwave them for 20-30 seconds. You can also heat them for 15 seconds on each side in a preheated skillet.
5. Stuff the tortillas with beef, onion relish, salsa, and cheese.
6. Serve with wedges of lime on the side.

Fish tacos

4 servings

Time to prepare: 10 minutes plus 30 minutes marinating

Time to cook: 7-10 minutes

Ingredients

1-pound fillet cod (or other flaky white fish), cut into 4 pieces

season with salt to taste

8 tortillas (fresh corn or flour)

Crema Mexicana (or substitute with sour cream)

Gallo Pinto

2 limes (quartered)

<u>To make marinated onion</u>

12 thinly sliced red onion

1 12 cup vinegar (red wine)

<u>For the marinade</u>

14 cup extra virgin olive oil

12 tsp ancho chilli powder

12 teaspoon oregano dried

12 teaspoon cumin powder

14 cup chopped lightly packed fresh cilantro leaves, plus more for garnish

1 jalapeno, peeled and diced

Directions

1. Marinate the onion for at least 30 minutes in the red wine vinegar. Set it aside for now.
2. Combine the marinade ingredients and marinate the fish for 20 minutes.
3. Preheat a nonstick skillet over medium-high heat. Put the fish in the pan and season it with salt. Allow it to cook for 4 minutes on one side, then flip it over and cook for another 2 minutes

93

on the other side. Take it out of the pan and flake it with a fork. If necessary, season with additional salt.

4. To heat the tortillas, wrap them in damp towels, 5 pieces at a time, and microwave for 20- 30 seconds. You can also heat them for 15 seconds on each side in a preheated skillet.
5. To make the tacos, spoon some of the marinated flaked fish into the centre of each tortilla. Serve with the marinated onions on top. Serve with cilantro garnished crema or sour cream and lime wedges.

MAIN ENTREES

Tex-Mex Beef Stew (Carne Guisada)

6 people

Time to Prepare: 10 minutes

Time to cook: 2 hours 15 minutes

Ingredients

3 pounds of chuck roast or shoulder, cut into chunks

3 tablespoons olive oil

1 large peeled and chopped onion

2 large seeded and chopped bell peppers

1/2 teaspoon salt

1 tsp pepper 1 tbsp garlic powder

1 teaspoon cumin

three tbsp flour

1/2 cup mild Rotel® tomatoes, chillies, or salsa

1/2 cups of water

2/3 cup tomato sauce

To serve, use flour or corn tortillas or plain rice.

Avocado slices or guacamole, shredded lettuce, and sour cream are optional toppings.

Directions

1. In a skillet over medium heat, heat the oil and brown the beef evenly (about 10 minutes).
2. Sauté the onion and bell pepper for 7 minutes, or until softened.
3. Cook until thickened, stirring in the salt, pepper, garlic powder, cumin, and flour (about 2 minutes).
4. Bring the Rotel® tomatoes/salsa and water to a boil.
5. Reduce to low heat, cover, and cook for 2 hours, stirring occasionally.
6. Cook for 15 minutes, or until the beef is tender enough to flake with a fork, after adding the tomato sauce.

7. Can be accompanied by tortillas, plain rice or Mexican rice, avocado slices or guacamole, shredded lettuce, and sour cream.

Fajitas de carne

4 servings

Time to prepare: 10 minutes plus 1 hour of marinating time

Time to cook: 15 minutes

Ingredients

1 medium yellow onion

1 Tbsp. vegetable oil

1 pound steak (flank or skirt)

3 assorted bell peppers, stemmed, seeded, de-ribbed, and sliced into strips lengthwise

Salt

8 flour tortillas (8 inches)

Shredded cheese, salsa, shredded lettuce, sour cream, and guacamole are among the toppings.

<u>To make the marinade</u>

One lime juice

2 teaspoons olive oil

2 garlic cloves, peeled and minced

12 teaspoon cumin powder

14 cup fresh cilantro, chopped 12 fresh jalapeno pepper, seeded

Directions

1. Peel and slice the onion with the grain rather than against the grain. Sections should be 12 inches wide at their widest point.
2. Make the marinade by combining all of the ingredients.
3. Refrigerate the steak for at least 1 hour before cooking. After marinating, remove the steak from the marinade and season with salt.

4   For 2 minutes, heat a large cast-iron pan or griddle over high heat. Heat for 1 minute after adding the oil. Cook the steak until it is medium-rare (about 3 minutes on each side).

5   If the oil reaches the smoking point, turn down the heat. Remove from the heat, tent (loosely cover) with foil, and set aside for 5 minutes. Keep the pan hot while you cook the vegetables.

6   If necessary, add a little more oil to the pan before adding the onions and bell peppers. Allow these to sear for 1 minute before stirring only occasionally for 5 minutes.

7   Thinly slice the meat against the grain.

8   Top with shredded cheese, salsa, shredded lettuce, sour cream, guacamole, and warmed flour tortillas and serve immediately.

Pork Chops Tex-Mex

Serves: 4

Time to Prepare: 10 minutes

Time to cook: 7 minutes

Ingredients

12-pound (4 pieces) bone-in pork loin chops

For the marinade

1 teaspoon brown sugar

2 teaspoons cumin powder

2 tablespoons chilli powder

1 teaspoon sea salt

1 Tbsp. vegetable oil

Directions

1. Combine the marinade ingredients and rub them on the pork chops. You can marinate the pork chops for up to 24 hours.
2. Preheat the grill to medium and lightly oil it.
3. Place the pork chops on the grill, cover, and cook for 5-7 minutes, flipping halfway through, or until done to preference.
4. Can be accompanied by corn, plain or Mexican rice, and guacamole.

Fideo (Mexican Spaghetti)

Serves 4 people.

Time to Prepare: 15 minutes

Time to cook: 20 minutes

Ingredients

two tbsp vegetable oil

1 package (8 oz.) fideo pasta

1/2 cup minced onion

2 minced garlic cloves

1 can (8 oz.) tomato sauce, divided

12 cup chicken broth or water

1 teaspoon cumin powder

1/2 tsp garlic salt

1 tsp chilli powder (or to taste)

1/2 teaspoons of sugar (optional)

grated queso fresco

Directions

1. In a saucepan over medium-high heat, heat the oil.
2. Cook until the video, onion, and garlic are browned.
3. Add half a can of tomato sauce and a cup of chicken stock or water. Stir in the cumin, garlic salt, and chilli powder to combine. Bring it to a boil and continue to cook until the liquid has almost completely evaporated.
4. Combine the remaining tomato sauce, sugar (optional), and chicken stock or water in a mixing bowl. Cook, covered, for about 10 minutes, or until the fideo is tender and the sauce has thickened.
5. Garnish with grated queso fresco before serving.

8 servings

Time to Prepare: 15 minutes

Time to cook: 15 minutes

Ingredients

2 refrigerated pizza dough tubes

12 cup salsa

2 cups smoked cheddar, shredded 4 mushroom caps, thinly sliced 2 tablespoons sliced pimento salad olives, drained 1 small onion, chopped 1 handful cilantro, chopped 12 small red bell pepper, seeded and diced 1 jalapeno, chopped 14 cup cilantro, chopped 12-pound chorizo, casing removed and thinly sliced

1 cup Monterey Jack cheese, shredded

Directions

1. Preheat the oven to 450 degrees Fahrenheit.
2. Form two pizza shells on two baking sheets.
3. Distribute the salsa evenly between the two pizzas.
4. Divide the smoked cheese among the bowls and top with the salsa.
5. Arrange the vegetables and chorizo on top of both pizzas, then top with the shredded Monterey Jack.
6. Bake for 15 minutes, or until the cheese is golden and the toppings are tender.

Fajitas with chicken

8 servings

Time to prepare: 15 minutes plus 10 minutes for overnight marinating

Time to cook: 35 minutes

Ingredients

1-pound skinless, boneless chicken breasts

Kosher salt or sea salt

black pepper, freshly ground

1 medium seeded and sliced into 12-inch strips of bell pepper

105

1 medium red onion, halved and cut into 12-inch slices

1 Tbsp. vegetable oil

8 corn or flour tortillas (6 inches)

Guacamole, salsa, lettuce, and sour cream (optional)

<u>To make the marinade</u>

13 cup coarsely chopped fresh cilantro

2 garlic cloves, finely chopped

12 tsp chilli powder

12 teaspoon coriander powder

12 teaspoon cumin powder

One lime juice

two tbsp vegetable oil

Directions

1. Combine the marinade ingredients. Marinate the chicken in the refrigerator for at least 10 minutes and up to overnight.
2. Preheat a grill pan to medium-high heat.
3. Season the chicken pieces with salt and pepper and place them on the grill.
4. Cook until well browned on one side (about 10 minutes).
5. Flip and season the second side with salt and pepper.

6. Cook, stirring occasionally until the other side is well browned (about 10 minutes).

7. Set the chicken on a cutting board to rest.

1. Meanwhile, in a medium mixing bowl, combine the bell pepper and onion, drizzle with 1 tablespoon of oil, season with salt and pepper, and toss to coat.

8. Arrange the vegetables in a single layer on the hot grill pan.

2. Cook until slightly charred, about 10 minutes (about 10 minutes). Transfer to a \sserving dish.

12. To heat the tortillas, wrap them in damp towels, 5 pieces at a time, and microwave for 20- 30 seconds. You can also heat them for 15 seconds on each side in a preheated skillet. To keep warm, wrap them in a towel.

13. Cut the chicken into strips or bite-sized pieces against the grain. Combine it with the vegetables in a serving dish.

14. Top with guacamole, salsa, shredded lettuce, and sour cream and serve with a warm tortilla.

Picadillo

Serves 6 people.

Time to Prepare: 15 minutes

Time to cook: 60 minutes

Ingredients

2 teaspoons olive oil

14 cup dried chorizo, diced 2 medium onions, peeled and chopped

4 garlic cloves, peeled and minced

12 lb. ground beef

108

To taste, season with kosher salt and freshly ground black pepper.

1 can (28 oz.) whole tomatoes, drained and crushed

2 tbsp vinegar (red wine)

1 tablespoon cinnamon powder

2 teaspoons cumin powder

two bay leaves

1 tsp ground cloves

1 tsp. nutmeg

13 cup raisin

13 cup stuffed pimiento olives

To serve, steamed rice

Directions

1. Heat the olive oil in a large, heavy skillet over medium-high heat until it shimmers.
2. Add the onions, chorizo, and garlic and cook until the onions begin to soften (about 10 minutes).
3. Cook until the ground beef is browned, breaking it up with a spatula. Remove any excess grease.
   Season with salt and black pepper to taste.
4. Combine the tomatoes, vinegar, cinnamon, cumin, bay leaves, cloves, and nutmeg in a mixing bowl.

109

5. Reduce the heat to low and cover for about 30 minutes.
6. Cook for another 15 minutes after adding the raisins and olives.
7. Toss with plain steamed rice and serve.

Chicken & Rice Bake

6 people can be served

Time to Prepare: 5 minutes

Time to cook: 45-50 minutes

Ingredients

1 medium chopped onion

1 teaspoon olive oil

1 package (6.9 oz.) chicken-flavoured rice and vermicelli mix

1-quart chicken broth

2 cup water

2 cups chopped cooked chicken or turkey

2 medium chopped and seeded tomatoes

3 tablespoons drained canned diced green chilli peppers

1 teaspoon crushed dried basil

1/2 teaspoon chilli powder

1/8 teaspoon cumin powder

1/8 tsp black pepper

1/2 cup cheddar cheese, shredded

Directions

1. In a medium saucepan, heat the oil over medium heat.
2. Cook the onion until it is tender.
3. Combine the rice and vermicelli mixture with the seasoning package in a mixing bowl.

111

1. Cook for 2 minutes, stirring constantly.
4. Bring the broth and water to a boil in a separate pot.
5. Reduce the heat to low, cover, and leave to cool for 20 minutes (not all of the liquid will be absorbed).
2. Preheat the oven to 425 degrees Fahrenheit.
6. Pour the rice mixture into a 2-quart casserole dish.
7. Combine the chicken, tomatoes, chilli peppers, basil, chilli powder, cumin, and black pepper in a mixing bowl. Cover with a lid or aluminium foil after thoroughly mixing.
8. Preheat the oven to 250°F and bake for 25 minutes.
9. Sprinkle with cheese and set aside to allow the cheese to melt.

Burger Tex-Mex

4 servings

Time to Prepare: 15 minutes

112

Time to cook: 12 minutes

Ingredients

1 halved, pitted and peeled avocado

1 teaspoon mayonnaise

3 tsp freshly squeezed lime juice

1 teaspoon hot sauce

Salt

1 seeded and diced plum tomato

1 tablespoon minced chipotle chilli in adobo

14 cup thinly sliced scallions

1 tablespoon minced fresh cilantro

<u>Burgers</u>

1/2 lb. lean ground beef

1/2 teaspoon chilli powder

1/2 teaspoon cumin powder

1/2 teaspoon oregano dried

Salt

113

4 oz. Monterey Jack or cheddar cheese

4 whole hamburger buns grilled to perfection

<u>as a garnish</u>

Jalapeno rings, pickled (bottled)

four lettuce leaves (preferably Boston bib lettuce)

Directions

1. In a mixing bowl, combine 14 the avocado with the mayonnaise, lime juice, hot sauce, and salt to taste. Using a fork, mash the potatoes until smooth.
2. Combine the tomato, chipotle, scallions, and cilantro in a mixing bowl.
3. Cut the remaining avocado into 14-inch cubes and fold into the vegetable mixture gently. Refrigerate after wrapping in plastic wrap.
4. To make the burger patties, lightly mix the chilli powder, cumin, oregano, and salt into the beef.
5. Divide the meat into four equal portions and shape it into patties with your hands.
6. Preheat a cast-iron skillet or grill pan over medium-high heat.
7. Cook the hamburgers to rare (about 5 12 minutes per side) when the pan or grill is hot.
8. Arrange the cheese slices on top of the patties and cook, covered, for 10 minutes to melt the cheese (about 1 minute).
9. Transfer the patties to a plate, tent with foil, and set aside for 3 minutes.
10. Place the patties on the buns (toasted or grilled, if desired).
11. Drizzle with avocado dressing and top with pickled jalapeno rings and lettuce.

DESSERTS

Caramel Flan

4 servings

Time to Prepare: 10 minutes

Time to cook: 25 minutes

Caramel-making ingredients

a 1/2 cup of sugar

2 teaspoons water

<u>To make the custard</u>

1-quart milk

1 tsp vanilla extract

two whole eggs

1/4 cups of sugar

1 teaspoon zest of lime (you may use orange or lemon zest instead)

Directions

1. In a saucepan, combine the sugar and water to make the caramel. Cook, stirring occasionally, over medium-high heat. Allow the sugar to melt and caramelize. When the syrup turns a deep amber colour, remove it from the heat and immerse the pan in cold water. (NOTE: Hot caramel can burn your skin.) Divide the caramel among four small ramekins. Place aside.
2. Preheat the oven to 350°F for the custard.
3. Heat the milk and vanilla in a medium-sized pot or saucepan over medium-high heat. As soon as the pot begins to boil, remove it from the heat.
4. In a separate bowl, whisk together the eggs and sugar. Pour the hot milk and vanilla mixture into the eggs and sugar in a thin stream, whisking constantly. Strain the mixture into a clean bowl using a fine-mesh strainer.
5. Divide the mixture evenly among the caramel-coated ramekins.
6. Arrange the ramekins in a shallow baking dish or on a baking sheet.
7. Fill the pan halfway with water, about halfway up the ramekins.
8. Bake for 30 minutes, or until a knife inserted into the centre comes out clean.
9. Remove the flans from the oven and set them aside to cool.

10. Wrap in plastic wrap and place in the refrigerator for 2 hours to overnight.
11. To remove the flan from the ramekin, use a small knife to cut around the edges and flip it onto a serving plate. Tap the ramekin's bottom until you hear the flan slide out.

Churros

4 servings

Time to Prepare: 10 minutes

Time to cook: 10 minutes

117

Ingredients

<u>To make the dough or paste</u>

1 cup of water

2 1/2 tbsp sugar

1/2 teaspoons of salt

two tbsp vegetable oil

1 cup unbleached all-purpose flour

frying oil

<u>Sugar with cinnamon</u>

1/2 cup granulated sugar

1 teaspoon cinnamon powder

Direction

1. In a mixing bowl, combine the cinnamon sugar ingredients, and
    Place it aside.
2   Combine the water, sugar, salt, and 2 tablespoons of vegetable oil in a mixing bowl.
    a small saucepan heated on medium heat
3   Bring it to a boil and then turn off the heat.
4   Stir in the flour constantly. Continue to mix until a paste-like dough forms.
5   Preheat the frying oil in a deep-fryer or deep skillet to 375°F.

118

6   Pipe strips of dough into the hot oil with a pastry bag.
7   Fry until golden on both sides and drain on paper towels.
8   Coat the drained churros in cinnamon sugar.
9   Distribute.

CONCLUSION

Change can be both exhilarating and overwhelming. Tex-Mex cuisine embodies both tradition and innovation. It is as dynamic as the fast-paced American way of life, preserving the best of the past while adding to the present. I hope you enjoy this collection of recipes and will return to them again and again. Fill in the blanks with whatever you can think of and come up with your unique creations. Experiencing the vibrant colours, textures, and flavours of Tex-Mex cuisine is a must!

9 783986 539122